Two Men Talk About Marriage

TWO MEN
talk about
MARRIAGE

Jeremy Bell and John McCaughan

Connor Court Publishing

Published in 2016 by Connor Court Publishing Pty Ltd

Connor Court Publishing Pty Ltd
PO Box 7257
Redland Bay QLD 4165
sales@connorcourt.com
www.connorcourt.com
Phone 0497-900-685

ISBN: 9781925501124

Cover design: Maria Giordano

Photo © Giovanni Portelli Photography

Printed in Australia

Acknowledgments

We are grateful to all the people who took the time to read and comment on drafts of this book: Jeremy Ambrose, Victoria Costello, Maria English, Elspeth Macpherson, Anthony Mason, Genevieve McCaughan, Emma O'Shea, and Gabrielle Williams. We are especially grateful to Catherine Pearce for her extensive feedback.

We would also like to thank Fr. Bill Milsted and Fr. Epeli Qimaqima for their support.

Contents

INTRODUCTION

We have written this book because we believe in 'traditional' marriage and wish to see it protected. But who are we?

We are two unmarried men from very different backgrounds. John is the second of eleven children and his parents remain happily married after thirty-three years. Jeremy is the eldest of two children, whose parents separated when he was nine and later divorced. John was raised Catholic and, despite a rocky patch in his early twenties, he has never abandoned his faith. Jeremy was not raised in any faith tradition and for some years was strongly anti-Christian. For most of his twenties he also considered himself exclusively homosexual, and for nearly five years he was in a relationship with another man. After many years of having no faith at all, he became a Catholic in his early thirties.

You might have expected us to end up on opposite sides of the marriage debate, given our vastly different upbringings and life-experiences. Yet we did not.

Although both of us are now practising Catholics, this is not a religious book. It so happens that, when each of us first thought seriously about the subject of marriage, religion barely came into it. John was at rock bottom career-wise, emotionally and spiritually, though still a believer. Jeremy was not even a believer. He had recently broken up with his partner, but had hopes of getting back together with him. He and his ex-partner had even talked of getting married. Nonetheless, his reflections on marriage led him in the same direction as John: towards the 'traditional' (one man, one woman) view of marriage.

This book is our attempt to explain why.

1

WHAT IS MARRIAGE?

"I love you!" We all want to say and hear these words. Love is our deepest need and, when found, our greatest joy. Love is the rallying cry for advocates of same-sex marriage – and, in a way, they are right. Sexual love finds its home in marriage. Two people in love naturally wish to make an exclusive, unconditional commitment to each other. Is there anything more to marriage than this? Advocates of same-sex marriage say no. Two men or two women can build a life together, "forsaking all others", just like husbands and wives. Why not then call a loving same-sex relationship a marriage?

The vision of marriage we would like to offer goes beyond loving mutual commitment, but we certainly do not want to downplay its importance. Most of us can agree that exclusive, unconditional commitment is at the heart of marriage. Indeed, what other relationship requires such commitment? We don't expect our friends, even our best friends, to forgo all other friendships. Nor is it necessary for friends to make any formal *promise* to remain friends. What makes marriage different? Why, in particular, do spouses make an *exclusive* commitment to each other?

When they exchange rings, each says, "Take this ring as a sign of my love and fidelity". Fidelity means, above all, sexual fidelity. The spouses promise not to share themselves sexually with anyone else. They promise not to cheat on each other. Why is this promise so important? Clearly we need an answer to this question if we want to understand what marriage is all about. And this means we need to understand what sex and marriage have to do with each other in the first place.

Sex, Love and Marriage

In 2009, a court in Nice granted a divorce to a couple whose 21-year marriage had been ruined, so the wife claimed, by her husband's unwillingness to have sex more often. The divorce court agreed with her, finding the sexually inactive husband 'solely responsible' for the relationship's breakdown. Two years later, the woman successfully sued her ex-husband for dereliction of marital duty. France's civil code stipulates that a married couple must 'share a communal life'. According to the judge in the case, this means that 'sexual relations must form part of a marriage'. She went on to say that "[a] sexual relationship between husband and wife is the expression of affection they have for each other, and in this case it was absent". If we take her at her word, the judge was here making a remarkably bold claim about marriage. A sexual relationship is *the* expression - the one and only expression - of marital affection! The unfortunate man was ordered to pay his ex-wife 10,000 euros in damages.[1]

---

1 "Husband Sued by Wife for Lack of Sex", *Sydney Morning Herald*, 6 September 2011, http://www.smh.com.au/lifestyle/life/husband-sued-by-wife-for-lack-of-sex-20110905-1juqw.html

We may not like the idea of a married couple's sex life being policed in this way, but we can sympathise with the woman's complaint. Sex is normally vital to a healthy marriage. Although the judge was rhetorically exaggerating when she called sex *the* expression of marital affection, it is of course a uniquely important one. Sexual intimacy expresses, as nothing else can, the special love that spouses have for each other. As the *Book of Common Prayer* has the husband say, "with my body I thee worship".

To be sure, it isn't obvious just why people who have this special love for each other should want to *marry*. After all, some committed sexual partners are happy just cohabiting, sometimes for a whole lifetime. Still, since people in love very often *do* want to marry, we might think there is no great puzzle about why sexual fidelity is so important in marriage. Two people marry because they love each other as they love no one else. More, they love each other in a way they *cannot* love anyone else. Romantic love is naturally and spontaneously 'exclusive', quite apart from marital vows. This is one reason why it is both so beautiful and, sometimes, so painful. Most of us have known the anguish of unrequited love. While it lasts, we cannot imagine feeling the same way about anybody except the one who, sadly, does not return our affection. The special way spouses express their special love for each other is sex. If one of them engages in extra-marital sex, it is as if he or she were saying to the other, "I love someone else, not you".

Why does Fidelity matter?

It might seem that little more needs to be said about marital
fidelity. However, matters are not so simple. For one thing,
unfaithful spouses sometimes care little or nothing for their
extra-marital partners. This is obvious in the case of one-
night stands. Yet even a one-off, loveless encounter with
another woman by an otherwise faithful husband may cause
deep and lasting damage to his marriage.

> (John) *I remember a conversation I once had with my then-
> girlfriend's father in the pub. He was uncharacteristically down,
> as one of his best friends was in serious marriage trouble. I
> remember his words vividly. "It was a one-night stand, so I get
> why she's pissed - but it was ten years ago and he's been with no-
> one else! At some point you just have to let it go! Forgive. Move
> on."*

Why should it be so difficult to 'move on'? Why should a
casual fling by a loving spouse cast a permanent shadow (or
worse) over his or her marriage? The unfaithful spouse breaks his
or her marital vow, of course, but the question is why this vow
is so important anyway. Cheating hurts, vow or no vow - anyone
whose boyfriend or girlfriend has been unfaithful knows that.
Spouses promise not to share themselves sexually with outsiders
because sexual exclusivity matters, not vice versa.

A normally faithful husband who has an unplanned one-
night stand with a stranger obviously does not want to wreck
his marriage. Perhaps he is often away from home on work trips,
lonely and in need of companionship. One night, feeling lonelier
than usual and fed up with his job, he gets talking to a friendly,
sympathetic woman. He suddenly craves a little 'harmless fun'.

And, as he leads her to his bedroom, he may try to persuade himself that this is indeed all they are doing: having some harmless, meaningless fun. He has no strong feelings for her and nor does she for him. Their transient sexual intimacy is not an expression of love on either side; it is just a brief spell of shared physical pleasure and, for him, a temporary escape from crushing loneliness. Why should this be a big deal?

If we think about it, this is a good question. After all, many of us at some point in our lives have sexual encounters just for pleasure. Countless people have sex without any thought of permanent attachment. Sexual desire seemingly has a life of its own, with no necessary connection to love. Indeed, considering the fire of sexual passion, a *permanent* and *exclusive* sexual commitment might seem unnatural. No matter how much we love someone, such a commitment might seem unrealistic. At least, it might seem unfair to expect *everyone* who has made such a commitment to stick to it rigidly.

Certainly, most people want to settle down sooner or later with just one person. Casual sex is fine for a time, we may feel, but a person cannot sow wild oats forever. From this point of view, a married man who has a one-night stand is refusing to shoulder the responsibilities that come with settling down. We can sympathise with him in his loneliness, but we feel bound to tell him that, at the end of the day, he really is behaving like an irresponsible teenager.

(John) *I used to get regular lifts in to work with my boss. Traffic leading to his office was chaotic at best so we'd often end up having conversations to pass the time. This particular day he was reminiscing about life in his twenties. "Sex, parties, ecstasy, it was all gooood! I had my fun. But like anything you eventually settle down." This last sentiment was echoed by his wife in a conversation we had some time later. She was telling me how much the community looked up to him. "He's honest, people always know he tells the truth and he's a good husband. We've been married for twenty years and he doesn't drink, he doesn't smoke and he doesn't chase other women."*

Suppose we take our lonely husband aside the day after his one-night stand and ask him why he did it. And suppose he digs in his heels. "It didn't mean anything! Before we got married, my wife and I both fooled around - and no one was hurt. No one will be hurt now if she doesn't find out. I'm hundreds of miles from home and miserable. I know it was wrong - it won't happen again." If we remind him that he promised to be faithful, he fires back: "So what? Everyone breaks promises sometimes. I still love my wife. Breaking a promise *once* doesn't make me a bad husband. And, frankly, I don't think I have been unfaithful – not really. In my heart, I'm 100 per cent committed to my wife. I would never even think of leaving her. Sex with her is special, and it's special *because it's all about love*. Last night wasn't about love! It was just sex. Okay, I know I shouldn't be having casual sex now that I'm married, and I won't do it again, but cut me some slack. Last night was stupid, but I wasn't *really* unfaithful."

Is he right that his one-night stand really did not mean anything – or, at least, that it meant nothing serious? If the meaning of sex were just a matter of the intentions and feelings of those involved, we could hardly disagree with him. *He* meant nothing by it; doesn't it follow that it really meant nothing, or anyway nothing serious? Well, clearly his wife would not see it this way!

Perhaps more importantly, he himself cannot quite bring himself to see it this way either. If he wholeheartedly believed it was meaningless, why did he need to defend himself? He wishes it *could* have been meaningless. He wishes it could have been just a quick snatch of harmless pleasure and relief from loneliness. Still, the hard truth is that it wasn't.

Can sex ever truly be meaningless?

Why is this? Why is it that married people *cannot* have 'meaningless' extra-marital sex, even if they occasionally wish they could? As we have seen, the answer is not just that having sex with someone else involves breaking a promise to one's spouse. In fact, it is the other way round. The point of the promise is that sharing oneself sexually with someone else would be wrong anyway. In other words, it is only *because* sex with a third party cannot be 'meaningless' that spouses make the promise never to engage in it. Likewise, committed unmarried partners usually recognise that, even without a formal exchange of vows, sexual exclusivity is a must.

We might want to say that, when two people fall in love, this naturally changes the way they feel about sex. Previously, perhaps, they could have casual, 'meaningless' sex with anyone they happened to like, but now they can't. Falling in love has made them take sex more seriously than they did before. This explains why spouses and informally committed partners embrace sexual exclusivity, doesn't it? In one way, yes - but, in another way, no. It is all well and good to say that a couple in love naturally take sex more seriously than they otherwise might, but this begs the question: *why* is it natural for them to do this? What is it that virtually *compels* a spouse to take extra-marital sex so seriously, even at those (hopefully rare) times when he or she is sorely tempted to pretend it wouldn't be a big deal?

Compare sex with kissing. When a woman kisses her husband, this is of course an expression of her special love for him. If he sees her kissing another man and interprets this as an expression of the same kind of love, he will feel betrayed. On the other hand, unless he is irrationally jealous, he will not give a moment's thought to her kissing another man who is just a good friend. A kiss can mean different things, and its meaning *will* sometimes depend on the feelings and intentions of the person giving it. But sex is not like this. If the husband were to catch his wife in bed with the other man, he would hardly be impressed at her assuring him, "we're just good friends"!

Does sex have an intrinsic meaning?

Sex seems, then, to have an *intrinsic* meaning – a meaning that is independent of, and even potentially in conflict with, the feelings and intentions of the parties involved. If this is right, it has important implications for marriage. The very nature of human sexuality seemingly makes it impossible for a spouse to have 'casual' extra-marital sex. But this in turn prompts the thought that sex *between* spouses can never be genuinely 'casual' either. This is not to say that sex in marriage cannot be simply pleasurable. Of course it can, and should be! But it always involves something more than carefree pleasure. Just as no one can sincerely say "I love you" altogether casually, so too no couple can 'make love' altogether casually. The specialness of sex is inescapable. And this surely means, more generally, that sex can never really be 'casual', whether between spouses, *de facto* partners or anyone else. Even the most light-hearted, 'no strings attached' sexual encounter, has something in it that sets it apart from all straightforwardly casual social encounters.

One sign of this is that, no matter how uninhibited we may be, most of us would shrink from the idea of having sex in public – and not just because we don't want to be arrested. We share food, talk, and hug each other in public. Most of us are quite happy to kiss in public. The climactic moment in many a wedding is when the groom lifts his bride's veil and kisses her in full view of the congregation. Some of us don't mind occasionally appearing naked in public, e.g., at nudist beaches. Yet nearly all of us draw a firm line at public sex, under any circumstances. (Admittedly, sex *in a public place* can have a certain thrill, but only if the participants have a real fear of being caught. If they were indifferent to being caught – if, that is, they honestly thought that sex in public was no big deal – they would not find it thrilling.) This near-universal taboo would make little sense if we were convinced deep down that sex can, even occasionally, be something genuinely casual.

Casual sex: is there such a thing?

Does this mean 'casual sex' is really a contradiction in terms? That is indeed what we are suggesting. The idea may seem far-fetched. After all, a great many people have unplanned sexual flings, with no deep feeling on either side and without subsequent regrets. How can we say that these are not 'casual'?

Unplanned flings are certainly casual *in spirit* but, as we have emphasised, it is a stubborn reality of sex that it has a meaning not fully within our control. Up to a point, it doesn't matter in what spirit we engage in it; our sexual acts may mean more than we intend. And most of us at some level know this.

Of course, we very often *want* sex just for pleasure, 'no strings attached'. Even men and women who have been happily married for years can unexpectedly find themselves eyeing an attractive stranger. As we remarked earlier, it can indeed seem simply *unnatural* for human beings to commit themselves permanently to an exclusive sexual relationship. Christopher Ryan, co-author of the 2010 best-seller *Sex at Dawn*, has bluntly declared that "all women are sluts, as are all men".[2] Human beings, in his view, are trousered apes yearning to shed their trousers.

Yet even if this were true, we don't think it would follow that exclusive sexual relationships are unnatural. Even if human sexual desire really were as naturally voracious and undiscriminating as that of chimps and bonobos, human sexuality would still have a dimension that ape sexuality lacks. We know that our sexual behaviour has a natural meaning absent from the sexual behaviour of apes. We know it can express a special kind of love, and we naturally long for this love. Although sexual exclusivity sometimes goes against our grain, true love is content with nothing less. And it is precisely because our natural sexual desires all too often urge us in a different direction that it makes sense for us to make a solemn *promise* not to share ourselves sexually with anyone except the man or woman we love. Far from being 'unnatural', the institution of

---

2 Ryan made this claim in a talk at Sydney Opera House on 28 June 2014, entitled "Is Monogamy Unnatural?". A transcript of the talk can be accessed at http://www.abc.net.au/radionational/programs/scienceshow/is-monogamy-unnatural3f/5516302#transcript.

marriage is solidly grounded in our natural needs. On the one hand, it respects our natural longing for a relationship based on sexual exclusivity. On the other, it takes due account of our natural inclination not to shoulder the responsibilities that come with such a relationship. This is one reason why sexual love finds its home, not simply in a relationship, but in a marriage.

Sexual love leading to new life: The wonder of parenthood

We are proposing that sex has an intrinsic, natural meaning, independent of our feelings and intentions. Clearly, if we are right, this meaning has a lot to do with the power of sex to express romantic love. However, we believe that any exploration of the meaning of sex must also consider its connection with reproduction.

Most of us, at some point in our lives, want children. Usually we envision raising them with our spouse or life-partner, but this need not be the case. Some people with no interest in marriage or romance still want children. Prospective first-time parents typically look forward to the birth of their child with eager impatience. Yet no matter how much they look forward to it, their emotion at the child's arrival often far surpasses their expectations.

> (Jeremy) *At the end of 2004, in the wake of my younger brother's death, my father began keeping a journal in which he reflected on his experience of fatherhood. He eventually showed it to me, and I will never forget his description of his feelings the day I was born. I was my parents' first child. They had been trying for some time to have kids and my mother had already suffered one intrauterine foetal death. There had been prolonged complications*

while she was pregnant with me, making them both fearful of a miscarriage. In the end, I was born premature. My father wrote of holding me in his hands for the first time. "As I lifted him up, the baby gave a strong cry of distress. I was suffused with joy. My life began in earnest at that moment. Everything before then had been frivolous, insubstantial."

Neither of the present authors is a father, so we cannot know just what it is like to see and hold a child of one's own for the first time. However, even without first-hand experience, anyone can grasp something of the unique wonder of parenthood. Although giving birth is a commonplace – hundreds of thousands of babies are born every day – it is nonetheless an act like no other. When we reflect on the many wonderful things of which men and women are capable, we normally think in the first instance of scientific, artistic, political, commercial and technological achievements. Young people who yearn to do great things and 'make a difference' dream of curing cancer or colonising outer space. Yet what product of human ingenuity and industry could possibly compare with human life itself? Bringing a new human being into the world is an incomparably greater act than painting the Mona Lisa or splitting the atom, even though it requires no special talents or skills.

What we mean by Parenthood

We wish to stress that we are talking about *biological* parenthood, not simply the assumption of responsibility for rearing a child. Adopting a child is undoubtedly a beautiful act and, in most cases, a source of deep joy to the adoptive parents. We would not think of suggesting otherwise. Again, it often happens that a child is raised by a couple, only one of whom is a biological parent. The lack of blood-relationship is no necessary obstacle to the biological parent's spouse or partner forming a deep and loving attachment to the child. Nonetheless, raising someone else's child is not the same as begetting a child of one's own. The authors are good friends with a married couple who adopted a baby girl two years ago and we have seen how it has transformed their lives. But they strove for some years to have children of their own, and it has been a source of deep grief to them that they were not ultimately able to do so. We do not think it unjust or unfeeling to note the simple and obvious truth that part of the matchless delight of parenthood is the knowledge that the child is one's own. It is natural not only to want children but to want to *have* children.

Love giving birth to Love

Even if sex did not come into it, bringing a child into the world would be an extraordinary act. If human beings reproduced asexually, like strawberries and starfish, it would still be true that generating new human life would be incomparably greater than any other act of which human beings are capable. But the connection between human parenthood and sex makes the act more extraordinary still. Sex expresses, as nothing else can, a special kind of love. A man and woman love each other in this special way, the woman falls pregnant and, nine months later, she gives birth. The newborn child is the flesh and blood of both of them. He or she is a living symbol of their loving sexual union. And, as parents, they now have a new object of love – but of a new kind of love.

The love that the child, in turn, will have for his or her parents is a different kind of love again. None of us feels quite the same way about siblings, friends, lovers or children of our own as we do about our parents. The couple's sexual love has led to the flowering of parental and filial love. Furthermore, if all goes well, the parents' love for their child will serve to reinforce and deepen their love for each other. These things are as familiar and commonplace as pregnancy and childbirth themselves. Yet we rarely reflect on the wondrous character of human sexual reproduction. We call sex 'making love', but do we realise just how fitting this expression is? It is hardly even a metaphor to say that, when human beings reproduce, love gives birth to love.

Reproduction without love

To be sure, pregnancy may result from sexual intercourse that is not, on either side, an expression of love. More tragically, even when the partners do love each other and wish to raise a family together, the blossoming of family love after the birth of a child may be thwarted. Parents may split up, or else become tired of each other but stay together for the sake of the children. Children may grow up with little experience of real parental affection or even, in extreme cases, as victims of various kinds of abuse. Families should be circles of the warmest and most generous love, but this is all too often not the case. Unhappy family life may in fact leave a legacy of lasting and savage hatred. Even when it does not, relations between parents and children may be profoundly fraught.

(Jeremy) *My two dearest friends in the world both had outwardly unremarkable upbringings by loving parents, but each has tortured relationships with his mother and father. One of them finds it all but impossible to confide in his parents, even about the most important things. He had a long-term girlfriend whom he hoped one day to marry, yet he never told them about her and he once confessed to me that his single greatest anxiety at the prospect of marriage was the thought of having to break the happy news to them. The other friend has recently gone so far as to move cities chiefly in order to get as far away from his parents as possible. As a child of divorced parents I envy them both the comparative stability of their upbringing, but they serve to remind me of the terrible stresses and strains that can plague even stable, 'ordinary' families.*

When we describe human reproduction as 'love giving birth to love', then, we are not ignoring the often harsh realities of family life. We have in mind the way things ideally should be, not the way they always are. In fact, we think the peculiar bitterness of unhappy family relationships in one way tells in favour of this description. Why would an unhappy family life leave such deep scars if we did not all have a burning need for a happy one? Simple, uninterrupted 'domestic bliss' may well not exist except in sentimental novels and Hollywood films, yet we long for it all the same and we know that, in some sense, it is what family life should be.

Children add another dimension to sex

Although loveless sexual encounters are common (and sometimes lead to pregnancy), it remains true that a couple are more faithful to the meaning of sex when they engage in it as a mutual expression and celebration of love. Suppose now that a loving couple have a child together and subsequently build a tolerably happy family life. Should we not acknowledge that reproduction and childrearing add another dimension to the meaning of their sex life? Their sexual intimacy not only expresses their love for each other, but also *expands* it, in the most glorious way imaginable.

The natural purpose of sex

We have talked a lot about the natural 'meaning' of sex. At this point we would like to start talking about the natural *purpose* of sex. When we speak of the 'meaning' of sex, we are really thinking about what sex is *for*. Sex is for pleasure, for the celebration of romantic love and for bringing new life into the world – or so we are suggesting. These three purposes of sex are naturally connected. In the best-case scenario, a couple in love have sex and later give birth to a child they will love and nurture, and who will love them in turn. The sheer physical pleasure of sexual intercourse is not somehow separate from the loving delight the man and woman take in each other. Nor is childbirth and family life a sort of accidental addendum to their lovemaking. Fundamentally, they are engaged in one single act, which we are calling 'love giving birth to love'. Physical pleasure, romance and the happiness of family life all belong to this one, amazing act. Each is part of the natural purpose of sex.

If this is true, it seems to follow that the connection between sex and reproduction is not just a brute biological fact. It somehow has an intrinsic meaning – a natural purpose. The connection is, of course, not a tight one. Sexual intimacy other than coitus will not lead to pregnancy. Sex cannot lead to pregnancy if the couple is infertile. Even sex between fertile partners does not, in most cases, lead to pregnancy. Nonetheless, the biological connection between sex and reproduction is obvious, and its looseness does not diminish its significance. A loving couple conceives a child; does this momentous event really tell us nothing at all about the meaning of the sexual act that led to it – and more generally, about the meaning of human sexuality as such? We think this is implausible. At the very least, the (loose) connection between sex and reproduction suggests something profoundly important about the natural meaning – the natural purpose – of sex.

But some readers will here be wondering whether we really have any right to say that human sexuality has this natural 'purpose'. After all, nearly all heterosexual couples sometimes have sex without wanting children. Indeed, many couples often go to a lot of trouble to make sure that their lovemaking does *not* lead to children. Who says that sex *has* to have this purpose? In fact, who says that sex has to have any natural 'purpose' at all? What does it even mean to say that human sexuality has a natural 'purpose'? Human biology is a wonderful feat of evolution and we can enjoy using our bodies in all sorts of ways, but does it make any sense to say that our sexuality has a 'purpose'?

These are fair questions. We will try to answer them in the next chapter.

2

LIVING IN HARMONY WITH NATURE

In the last chapter, it was suggested that our sex lives have a meaning partly beyond our control. A husband's one-night stand with a stranger is not meaningless, even if he wants it to be. The possibility of pregnancy reveals something about the meaning of sexual intercourse, even though couples often have sex without wanting children. No matter how we feel about it, sex has an intrinsic significance that is not up to us.

It was further suggested that, when we talk about the natural meaning of sex, we are really talking about the natural *purpose* of sex. We are talking about what sex is naturally *for*. But this idea can seem bizarre. What sense can we make of the idea that parts of our bodies are 'for' this or 'for' that? Who says that our bodies have natural 'purposes' at all?

Nature and Science

Suppose we were to ask a biologist whether she thinks that body parts have 'purposes'. She might respond: "Certainly they do! The heart's purpose is to pump blood; the kidneys' purpose is to filter the blood and remove wastes from it; the purpose of the teeth is to tear and grind food so we can swallow it etc." And if we were then to ask her about the purpose of the male and female sexual organs, she would probably say: "Well, reproduction, obviously. They're even called 'reproductive organs', aren't they?" Clearly there is *some* sense in talking about the natural 'purposes' of our body parts, and in particular about the reproductive 'purpose' of our sexual organs.

Still, this is not quite what we had in mind in the last chapter. We talked about the natural 'purpose' of sex, but also about its natural 'meaning'. A biologist wouldn't be likely to talk about the 'meaning' of the heart's pumping or the teeth's chomping. Again, a biologist probably wouldn't say that part of the 'purpose' of sex is to celebrate romantic love.

Why is this? It is because biologists treat human beings simply as highly complex animals. A biologist is not normally interested in human needs and wants that go beyond animal drives and appetites. Biology does not investigate the *spiritual* side of human nature. When we talked about 'meaning' and 'purpose' in the last chapter, we were using spiritual language. Biology does not investigate human spirituality.

Humans are uniquely spiritual

Some readers might object to our using the word "spirituality", because it sounds religious. But we are not talking about anything specifically religious. We are talking about something that religious and non-religious people alike can agree sets human beings apart from other animals and makes them uniquely special. Human beings are capable of understanding concepts like 'good', 'evil', and 'beauty'. They are able to feel sentiments like shame and awe. Non-human animals lack these capacities. When a shark kills a surfer we are horrified, but we do not say that the shark has done something *wicked*, as we might say that a hit-and-run driver has done something wicked. A female peacock can be instinctively attracted by the male's magnificent plumage, but only a human being can detachedly admire the plumage for its own sake. A cat or a dog can be terrified by a thunderstorm, but only a human being can gaze, awestruck, at flashes of lightening and fancy that they are the work of angry gods. All of these examples are connected. They all manifest the fundamental difference between human beings and non-human animals. And we think the best way to express this difference is to say that human beings alone are spiritual animals.

Human sexuality reflects our spiritual nature

Human sexuality too reflects human spirituality. Chimps, dolphins and other animals have sex lives in some respects comparable to ours. They give every sign of having strong feelings of affection for their sexual partners. Some, like gibbons, even practice 'monogamy'. But animals do not make formal promises, with witnesses, of sexual fidelity. Gibbons presumably do not struggle guiltily with feelings of attraction to other gibbons that are not their 'spouses'. It seems absurd to talk of a male chimp 'cheating' on his mate, in the same sense that a human husband may cheat on his wife. It is only human beings who can be unfaithful to their sexual partners. Again, only human beings can reflect on the beautiful connection nature has established between lovemaking and childbirth. This connection, we are suggesting, has a spiritual significance. When a biologist says that the purpose of an animal's sexual organs is reproduction, she is not claiming that this biological fact has any spiritual significance. But we are claiming that, in the case of human beings, it *does*. Nature has given human lovers the capacity to create new life and new love in the very act by which they celebrate their existing love. Nature has made it possible for human reproduction to take on the miraculous character of 'love giving birth to love'.

But some readers will here protest vigorously. How *could* brute biological facts have a spiritual significance? This seems nonsensical. And why should we talk of nature 'giving' human beings anything? This makes it sound as if 'nature' were a living, intelligent thing! Aren't we just being sentimental if we talk this way? At the end of the day, aren't biologists quite right not to read any 'spiritual' significance into human anatomy?

Science is silent on spirituality

Let us take a step back for a moment. It is true that biologists, like other scientists, don't read any spiritual significance into the natural world. Or rather, they don't believe it is their business, *as scientists*, to read any spiritual significance into the natural world. Some scientists, in fact, do believe that nature is in some sense suffused with spiritual significance. Albert Einstein wrote of the "sublimity and marvellous order" manifested in nature, inspiring what he called a "cosmic religious feeling".[3] The great American astronomer Carl Sagan marvelled at the "intricacy, beauty, and subtlety of life" revealed by scientific research, and went so far as to describe science as "a profound source of spirituality".[4] Some scientists who are not conventionally religious even believe that there is literally *a spirit* at work in nature. Though disbelieving in a personal God, Einstein claimed that "[e]veryone who is seriously involved in the pursuit of science becomes convinced that a spirit is manifest in the laws of the Universe – a spirit vastly superior to that of man, and one in the face of which we with our modest powers must feel humble".[5] Nonetheless, he did not claim that science can *prove* that this superior spirit exists. He would never have dreamed of publishing a paper in a reputable scientific journal arguing for the existence of such a spirit. Scientists who take spirituality seriously still don't think that they should talk about it when doing science. Erwin Schrödinger flatly declared that "the scientific picture of the real world around me... is ghastly silent about all and sundry that is really near to our heart, that really matters to us".[6] This world picture "knows nothing of beautiful and ugly, good or bad, God and eternity". The scientific picture of the world says nothing about spirituality.

3 Albert Einstein, "Religion and Science", in *Ideas and Opinions* (New York: Crown Publishers, 1954), p.38

4 Carl Sagan, *The Demon-Haunted World: Science as a Candle in the Dark* (London: Headline, 1997), p.32

5 Albert Einstein, *Albert Einstein, The Human Side: New Glimpses from His Archives*, selected and edited by Helen Dukas and Banesh Hoffmann (Princeton, N.J. & Chichester, West Sussex: Princeton University Press, 1979), p.33

6 Erwin Schrödinger, *Nature and the Greeks* (Cambridge: Cambridge University Press, 1954), p.93

Our world without the spiritual:
The strictly scientific view of the world

So what is the non-spiritual, strictly scientific picture of the world? Crudely speaking, it is something like this: the universe consists of countless billions of unfathomably small elementary particles in ceaseless motion. All the things we see around us – mountains, rivers, plants, animals, buildings etc. – are, at bottom, just massive collections of these particles, temporarily held together by various forces. Scientists can discover the laws that govern the movements of all these particles. At the super-atomic level, at least, these laws are never broken. If we had enough information, we could predict with near-certainty the future course of every single atom from this moment onwards. In other words, we could predict the whole future of the whole visible universe.

Biologists would add to this general picture some observations about plants and animals. Billions of years ago, collections of elementary particles came together in such a way as to form the first primitive living beings. These organisms were able to replicate themselves, but subsequent generations were not always perfect copies. Random mutations sporadically occurred during the reproductive process, some of which turned out to give the mutants an edge in the struggle for survival. These mutations would then be passed on to the mutants' descendants, which would eventually become new species. And this laborious process was repeated over and over again. In this way, primitive species were able to evolve gradually into more complex ones. Over hundreds of millennia, the first living beings evolved bit by bit into far more complex life-forms – including, eventually, human beings. Our bodies are thus products of a long and seemingly random process of evolution.

There does not seem to be much room in the scientific worldview for what we are calling 'spirituality'. Certainly there does not seem to be any room in it for a spiritual attitude towards the human body. We have suggested that the human reproductive system has a spiritual significance. But what does science say about it? A human being's reproductive system is, on one level, just a temporary conglomeration of elementary particles, which came together in accordance with the laws of physics and chemistry. At another level, it is the end product of a haphazard, blind and apparently 'meaningless' evolutionary process. Either way, how can we say that it has any 'spiritual' significance?

We have already remarked that some scientists see no conflict between science and spirituality. Carl Sagan's description of science as "a profound source of spirituality" was no doubt sincerely meant. However, it seems plain that this description needs to be taken with a grain of salt. Science could only be a 'source of spirituality' to someone who did not rely solely *on* science for all of his beliefs. If all our ideas about the world (and about ourselves) were taken from science, our outlook on life would have no spiritual content. If the universe is, at bottom, a meaningless cosmic dust storm, spirituality has no place in it.

Do we need spirituality?

Some people might at this point be inclined to say 'So what? Who needs 'spirituality'? Science explains the world and enables us to have long and enjoyable lives. Why shouldn't we junk 'spirituality' and cheerfully accept a bare-bones, scientific world view?"

Think about what this would mean. If science tells us everything there is to know about the world and ourselves, it can start to look as if some of the things we care about most deeply are based on illusions. Take romantic love, for instance. What would a scientist say about love? Here is what one theoretical physicist, Jim Al-Khalili, has to say:

> *Biologically, love is a powerful neurological condition like hunger or thirst, only more permanent... [L]ove is basically chemistry... [I]n true love, or attachment and bonding, the brain can release a whole set of chemicals: pheromones, dopamine, norepinephrine, serotonin, oxytocin and vasopressin. However, from an evolutionary perspective, love can be viewed as a survival tool – a mechanism we have evolved to promote long-term relationships, mutual defence and parental support of children and to promote feelings of safety and security.*[7]

In the scientific worldview, love is at one level 'basically chemistry', comparable to hunger or thirst. At another level it is 'a survival tool', like a polar bear's thick fur coat or a cobra's venom. This seems an impoverished view of love, to say the very least. When a man makes his marriage vows, promising to 'love and honour' his wife all the days of his life, he takes himself to be promising to do more than regulate his body's chemical secretions for the next forty years or more. Love poets do not write odes to neurological conditions and survival mechanisms. It is striking that Al-Khalili claims to describe what love is, yet does not even mention that love is always love *for another human being*! If we accept his description, a person could be 'in love' – in

---

7 "What is love? Five theories on the greatest emotion of all", *The Guardian*, 13 December 2012, http://www.theguardian.com/commentisfree/2012/dec/13/what-is-love-five-theories

other words, in a certain neurological or biochemical condition – even if he had been raised in a laboratory by robots and had never met another human being. Like Keanu Reeves' character in *The Matrix*, he could be locked in a vat, with multiple tubes and electrodes plugged into his brain and glands, thanks to which the right chemicals are released and he 'falls in love'. But this is clearly nonsense. If science gives us a *complete* account of reality, it is hard not to think that 'true love', as we normally conceive it, must be a sort of pre-scientific delusion.

Love as biochemistry: How it looks in practice

If we understand 'love' along the lines Al-Khalili recommends, can we hold on to the notion that lovers have an *obligation* to be sexually faithful to each other? It is not obvious that we can. What connection could there be between a 'powerful neurological condition' and a duty of sexual fidelity? If a married man has a one-night stand and his wife finds out, she will no doubt feel terrible. That is, her brain will release plenty of chemicals that leave her feeling terrible. Perhaps the man's brain will release chemicals that leave him feeling pretty bad too. But where does the idea of duty or fidelity come in here? After all, scientists could probably design drugs to counteract these chemical effects. An unfaithful husband and a betrayed wife could take these drugs, feel better and get on with their lives, without resentment or guilt. The specifically moral notions of 'duty' and 'fidelity' seem at this point to lose their grip and vanish into thin air. And what becomes of 'true love', if there is no duty to be faithful to one's beloved?

The difficulties do not end there. When the married man decided to have a casual fling with a stranger, this decision itself must have had a physiological explanation. Presumably his brain released certain chemicals, causing him to hanker after some 'harmless fun', and off he went. We remarked earlier that, on the scientific worldview, unchanging laws of nature govern every event at the super-atomic level. These same laws governed all of the man's actions – his talking to the strange woman, his taking her hand and leading her to his bedroom etc. The motions of the many trillions of molecules that make up his body at any moment are always subject to these laws and can never violate them. A scientist who knew enough about the state of his body and his environment at the moment before he started talking to the woman could, in theory, have predicted his impending infidelity. In short, the man could not have felt or acted otherwise than he did. But does it make any sense to say that he has a duty not to be unfaithful, if he *could not help* being unfaithful?

Consider a more dramatic case. The notorious Josef Fritzl held his daughter Elisabeth captive for twenty-four years and fathered seven children with her. All of us would say without hesitation that this was monstrously wicked. Yet, in the scientific worldview, nature was simply taking its course. Fritzl's brain released pheromones, dopamine, norepinephrine, and so on, it sent electrical signals to his muscles, and the rest is history. When he repeatedly raped his daughter, the molecules composing his body and hers changed places in accordance with the laws of physics and chemistry – and, it would seem, that is really all there was to it. Does a complex rearrangement of trillions of organic molecules have a 'meaning'? And if, during those twenty-four years of Elisabeth's nightmarish imprisonment, nature was just taking its necessary, law-governed course in the Fritzl household, can we seriously maintain that Josef Fritzl was morally responsible for what he was doing?

Is life meaningless?

We began this chapter by considering the idea of biological 'purpose'. A biologist, we remarked, would probably be happy to speak of body parts, including the sexual organs, as having 'purposes'. At this point we would suggest, however, that a biologist who accepts the bare-bones scientific worldview has no real right to speak of biological 'purpose' in anything like the sense that we normally give this word. If the universe consists fundamentally of elementary particles in ceaseless, *purposeless* motion, what can it mean to say that the heart, for instance, has the 'purpose' of pumping blood? All it can really mean is that, at some point in the distant past, a series of accidental mutations resulted in the emergence of living beings with organs that, most of the time, pumped blood through their bodies. These organs, which we would in retrospect call 'hearts', turned out to increase the creatures' long-term chances of survival. Consequently, their descendants now exist in greater numbers, and have longer lives, than if the original series of accidental mutations had not occurred. Biologists may find it convenient to say that the heart has the 'purpose' of pumping blood, but the truth is that this is just a loose, dispensable metaphor. Strictly speaking, science has no need of the concept of 'purpose'.

A worldview based solely on the findings of science cannot accommodate what we are calling human spirituality. Goodness, wickedness, true love - none of these make sense in this worldview. Even biological 'purpose' makes no sense in this worldview, except as a colourful metaphor. If science told us the complete truth about reality, we would have to conclude that many of the things we care about most deeply are based on illusions. Consequently, if we were resolutely honest with ourselves, we would have to embrace what is sometimes called nihilism – the belief that life is meaningless. This is not a pleasant thought. Most of us do not want to be nihilists.

Nature and Spirituality

If we want to avoid nihilism, we have to reject the bare-bones scientific worldview. This does not mean that we have to turn our backs on science. It simply means that we need to acknowledge that there are dimensions of reality about which science has nothing to say. The world is more than just a mass of elementary particles in motion. But what is this 'more'? What is the alternative to the nihilist worldview?

Free will

We suggest, firstly, that there has to be room in a non-nihilist worldview for human free will. In other words, the laws of nature discovered by physicists and chemists may indeed explain most of the happenings in the world, but they cannot explain all of them. At least sometimes, human beings are free to act in one way *or* in another. No matter what involuntary chemical secretions and electrical impulses took place in his body, Josef Fritzl did not *have* to imprison and rape his daughter. He *could* have acted differently, if he had chosen to do so.

Although many philosophers and scientists deny the existence of free will, there is nothing necessarily 'unscientific' or anti-scientific about believing in it. Scientists understandably tend to assume that, when they discover some pattern in natural events, this pattern *must* be an instance of a universal law of nature that admits of no exceptions. They also tend to assume that *every* natural event must have a scientific explanation in terms of such universal, exceptionless laws. It follows from these two assumptions that human free will cannot exist. But why should we necessarily accept either of these assumptions? No scientist would claim to be able to reconstruct even a tiny fraction of the chemical and electrical events that must have taken place in Fritzl's body during his twenty-four-year abuse of his daughter. Why, then, shouldn't we suppose that at least some of his actions were *not* determined exclusively by the laws of physics and chemistry but were rather under his own voluntary control?

Natural goodness

Belief in free will, we maintain, is one essential feature of any robustly *non*-nihilist worldview. A second essential feature is the belief that some things are *naturally good*. The beauty of a peacock's plumage is something naturally good. The human capacity to celebrate romantic love through sexual intimacy is naturally good, though in a different way. The generation of new life, above all of new human life, is a uniquely great natural good. This idea of 'natural goods' may seem very simple and straightforward. Who would deny that beauty, sexual love and life itself are naturally good? But the idea is not quite as simple as it first appears. We have already seen the limitations of a purely scientific view of nature. The concept of 'goodness' plays no role in science. Elemental particles swirling blindly through space clearly cannot have more than an accidental connection with goodness. If we call something *naturally* good – good 'by nature' – we cannot be talking about 'nature' in exactly the same sense that a scientist would.

So what are we talking about? How could there be such a thing as 'natural' goodness, or goodness 'by nature'? Another way of putting the question is this: how could nature have any *non-accidental* connection with goodness?

Mother Nature and her mishaps

There seems to be only one possible answer to this question. Natural processes, or anyway some of them, must *aim* at goodness. Naturally good things must somehow be the *goals* of the natural processes that lead to them. Once a human sperm has fused with a human ovum, it is not enough to say that the ensuing nine-month process within the woman's body predictably leads to the birth of a human baby. The process *aims* at the baby's birth. A miscarried pregnancy is not just a tragedy for the parents; it is a failure on nature's part. If this is the case, then nature is not just matter in blind motion, as a scientist would suppose. In some cases, at least, nature is matter in *motion directed towards a goal*.

This suggestion may sound bizarre. Saying that some natural

processes have 'aims' or 'goals' again makes it sound as if nature is an intelligent being. As we said earlier, this is certainly not our view. We think that natural processes can meaningfully be said to have goals, even though the elementary particles involved in these processes clearly do not possess any kind of intelligence. This idea is not as foreign to our ordinary habits of thought as it might seem. People quite often talk as if nature had goals. Organic agriculture, for instance, is praised on the ground that it is 'farming as nature intended', and vegetarianism is recommended on the grounds that nature did not 'intend' human beings to eat meat. The notion that nature 'intends' or 'aims at' some things and not others is familiar to all of us.

It might be objected that talk of nature 'intending' this or that is obviously just figurative. But is it? Of course people who speak of 'farming as nature intended' do not think that the soil, the rain and the crops *want* human beings to farm in a certain way. That would be nonsense. But the champions of farming 'as nature intended' are convinced (rightly or wrongly) that the more farmers rely on nature, the better the results are likely to be. Perhaps without realising it, they are assuming that whatever is 'natural' *must* be good. Vegetarians who claim that they are living 'as nature intended' are making the same assumption. And this assumption, we are suggesting, only makes sense if we suppose that nature somehow *aims* at goodness.

The notion that whatever is natural *must* be good is, in fact, hugely popular in today's world. The explosion in demand for organic foods, 'natural' remedies and 'environmentally friendly' technology is of course partly based on straightforwardly utilitarian considerations, but it also reflects a deep-seated, if vague, sense of the basic goodness of nature. Many nudists reject clothing as 'unnatural', hence bad. (Some actually call themselves 'naturists'.) There are even people who decide to abandon civilisation altogether and try to live in the uncultivated wilderness, like the ill-fated Christopher McCandless, whose story is the subject of Sean Penn's film *Into The Wild*. We may well find some of these examples ludicrous or tragic. But we can understand the sentiments behind them.

All the same, can we seriously believe that nature sometimes 'aims' at goodness? Let us return to the example of pregnancy. It is surely not nonsense to say that pregnancy has the good of new life as its natural *goal*, not just as its usual natural upshot. If this makes sense, we may reasonably be open to the possibility that other natural processes likewise have natural goals. One obvious example is the process of healing after a wound. It makes good sense to suppose that the clotting of blood, the inflammation of the affected area and so forth have the natural goal, not just the natural result, of repairing the damage caused by the wound.

If natural bodily *processes* can meaningfully be said to have goals, then surely *parts* of the body can meaningfully be said to have purposes. The protein fibrin in the blood exists, partly, so that blood can clot and wounds can heal. Healing is one thing that fibrin is *for*. The male and female sexual organs come into being, partly, for the purpose of reproduction. Reproduction is one thing that they are for.

Moreover, why should we suppose that nature's goals must in every case be the maintenance or propagation of life and health? Nature has endowed human beings not only with sexual organs but also with organic chemicals such as dopamine and norepinephrine. These chemicals may not completely explain the emotions we feel when we are in love, but they clearly have something to do with them. The capacity of sexual intimacy to express romantic love might then be one of nature's goals in fashioning human sexuality – even apart from the connection between sex and reproduction. Again, the sheer beauty of the peacock's plumage might be one of the goals of its growth (and regrowth after moulting). If it makes sense to speak of nature having 'goals' at all, there is no obvious reason why the *only* goal of this particular process should be to ensure that the peacock finds himself a peahen.

Natural purpose: too much to believe?

But sceptics may here think that we are going much too far. How can any scientifically literate human being take seriously the idea that nature might aim at producing beauty, simply for its own sake? We suggest that, while this scepticism is understandable, it largely reflects the grip of the bare-bones scientific worldview on the contemporary imagination. Let us assume that human spirituality is not a mere phantom. In other words, let us assume that such things as beauty, morality and romantic love are more than pre-scientific delusions. Few would want to deny this. Now human beings are themselves products of nature. They belong to the natural world. It would therefore be very strange if nature contributed nothing at all to human spirituality. The existence of a spiritual side to human nature gives us good reason to think that spirituality cannot be wholly foreign to the natural world generally. To be sure, as we have already stressed, human beings alone are spiritual animals.

That is to say, human beings alone are capable of *understanding* spiritual realities, and acting in light of this understanding. Dogs and chimps cannot appreciate beauty or make and break promises. But this does not mean that the non-human natural world cannot in any way partake of spirituality. If we are prepared to accept that spirituality must in some way be present even in non-human nature, why should we not take seriously the idea that nature sometimes aims to produce beauty, just for its own sake?

A non-nihilist worldview, we have claimed, must accept that at least some natural processes have natural goods for their *goals*. This means, we are now claiming, that even the non-human natural world must somehow partake of spirituality. Indeed, the spirituality of the non-human natural world *grounds* our own spirituality, since we are products of nature. If this is right, it has important implications for how we should live our lives. We have free will, which we can use well or badly. If we are to use it well, we need to know what is naturally good. To some extent, we should seek to *live in harmony with nature*.

Life in Harmony with Nature

'Living in harmony with nature' – we hear this phrase often. What does it mean? In part, of course, it means living in a way that does not irreparably damage the natural world on which we depend. But, as we are trying to show it also has a deeper meaning. Human societies not in the grip of a bare-bones scientific view of the world have recognised this. Australia's indigenous inhabitants are often said to have learnt how to 'live in harmony with nature', prior to European settlement. They developed complex and sophisticated ecological practices over thousands of years (fire-stick burning, agriculture and animal husbandry, etc.), which have enabled them not only to survive this country's harsh and inhospitable conditions but also to cultivate and improve the natural environment. However, as is well known, they do not look upon their relationship with the natural world from a merely utilitarian point of view. They see it rather as a spiritual relationship. They believe they have a spiritual connection to the natural world in general, and to the land in particular. The land is not, for them, a mere resource to be exploited, but a sacred inheritance to be treasured and safeguarded. Moreover, they believe that they in some sense *belong* to the land. Indeed, on this view, everything that exists – including us – belongs to an ordered, meaningful whole, what the ancient Greeks called a 'cosmos'. 'Living in harmony with nature' means respecting the natural order and one's place in it.

Similar conceptions are found in other cultures too. Chinese Taoism teaches that the right 'way' (*tao*) of living is a way somehow in harmony with the natural world. Hinduism and Buddhism both recognise a principle of order and harmony (*dharma*) underlying the apparent chaos and randomness of natural events. The ancient Stoics strove to live 'according to nature' and went so far as to speak of a natural *law*, which humans must obey if they are to flourish and be happy. Even in the contemporary West, as we have already observed, the desire to 'get back to nature' is widespread and powerful. People often speak of 'Mother Nature', as if nature were a loving parent to whom we owe filial obedience.

Belief in a natural order imbued with spiritual significance will often, of course, go together with belief in some transcendent, intelligent being *above* this natural order, yet manifested *in* it. According to Black Elk, of the Native American Oglala Lakota tribe:

> *We should understand well that all things are the work of the Great Spirit. We should know that He is within all things: the trees, the grasses, the rivers, the mountains, and all the four-legged animals, and the winged peoples; and even more important, we should understand that He is also above all these things and peoples. When we do understand all this deeply within our hearts, then we will fear and love, and know the Great Spirit, and then we will be and act and live as He intends.*[8]

Some Christians combine the Stoic belief in 'natural law' with faith in God as supreme spirit and creator of nature. But even those of us who do not believe in God or in any 'Great Spirit' above nature can still believe in something like natural law. That is, we can still take seriously the idea that the natural world is somehow suffused with spirituality, and that human beings should seek to live 'in harmony with nature'.

Some readers will probably be wondering just what, concretely, 'living in harmony with nature' is supposed to involve. Up to a point, we would say, it involves nothing especially grand. We recognise certain things as naturally good and pursue them. Health, for instance, is a natural good. To live healthily is to live according to nature. Our natural appetites and aversions are largely reliable guides to healthy living: we should eat only to sate hunger, there should be a certain variety in our diet, we should

---

8 Black Elk, *The Sacred Pipe: Black Elk's Account of the Seven Rites of the Oglala Sioux*, ed. Joseph Epes Brown (Norman: University of Oklahoma Press, 1989), p.xx

avoid rancid food, we should try to avoid contact with excrement, we should get regular sleep, and so on. This certainly does not entail that the means we use to preserve or restore health must never be 'artificial'. Man-made medicine can sometimes restore a sick person to health when nature alone is unable to do so. Since health is a *natural* good, medicine here serves as an aid to one of nature's own goals. The same can be said about all human inventions, provided they are at the service of natural goods. It would be foolish to suppose that living 'according to nature' must mean fleeing civilisation and huddling naked in a cave with roots and raw flesh to eat. Our intelligence is part of our nature, and to spurn its marvellous fruits – technology, the arts, and civilised life in general – would be to live *unnaturally*.

What, now, would it mean to live our sex lives in harmony with nature? This will be the subject of the next chapter.

3

NATURAL MARRIAGE

A happy and flourishing life is one lived 'in harmony with nature' or 'according to nature'. This is what we have proposed. It is hardly a new idea, and we have tried to show why we think it deserves to be taken seriously. If it is right, how does it bear on sexuality? What is sex, and marriage, 'according to nature'?

Purpose and pleasure

Before tackling this question head-on, let us try to get our bearings by thinking about a similar, but much less emotionally and politically charged question: what is *eating* 'according to nature'? Eating is like sex in two important ways. It affords us great physical pleasure, and its most important purpose is the maintenance of life, as the most important purpose of sex is the generation of new life. If we understand what it means to eat according to nature, we will be in a better position to understand what it means to live our sex lives according to nature. Yet it may seem odd to ask what eating 'according to nature' might be. Obviously the purpose of eating is to stay alive, so eating according to nature means eating healthily – and that is pretty much all that needs to be said, isn't it? As we shall see, however, more can be said.

When the Roman Empire was near collapse, so it has been alleged, decadent Roman nobles would hold banquets at which they would eat till full, and then induce vomiting. Having emptied their stomachs, they could start eating again. In this way, they could enjoy the pleasure of a rich meal twice or even three times over in one night. This distasteful practice, known as the *vomitorium*, is in fact probably a myth. However, myth or not, it is worth reflecting on why we find the alleged practice repellent. Vomiting of course is not pleasant, but this is not the full story. If we accidentally ingest food that is poisonous, we may induce vomiting in order to expel the toxins. While disagreeable, this is clearly very different from the Roman practice. What is peculiarly distasteful about the *vomitorium*, we suggest, is the wilful separation of the pleasure of eating from its proper purpose, nourishment. Much as we enjoy our food and drink, we know that eating and drinking are above all a matter of staying alive and keeping healthy. "Eat to live, don't live to eat." Even simple over-eating for the sheer pleasure of it is distasteful. Eating and then vomiting out one's food before it is digested so as to have the appetite for more is twisted.

Physical pleasure, like other gifts of nature, can truly be said to have a purpose. Nature intends us to take pleasure in eating –

but only in eating directed to *its* basic purpose, nourishment. If it was real, the Roman *vomitorium* was an abuse of the pleasure of eating.

Consider another perverted kind of eating: cannibalism. Almost all human beings find cannibalism not just revolting but monstrous. Most of us see nothing wrong in blood transfusions and organ transplants, yet we feel disgusted at the very idea of drinking human blood and eating human flesh. To be sure, there are desperate situations in which cannibalism becomes necessary for survival. In 1972, a plane crashed in the Andes, killing some of the passengers. The others were eventually forced to eat parts of their dead companions to stay alive. We would probably say they did the right thing. Yet even forty years later, one of them described his act as 'repugnant'[9] – and who would disagree?

Our horror at cannibalism reveals something about our attitude towards the human body. We regard human bodies – even dead ones – as more than mere lumps of ingestible matter. We know that corpses decompose and quickly become unrecognisable. Even skeletons disintegrate eventually. The molecules of our distant ancestors are now parts of rocks, plants, animals, and even, perhaps, us. Yet we still treat a dead human body as more than just a mass of molecules awaiting redistribution. Why do we have elaborate and expensive ceremonies for burying or cremating our loved one's bodies? It would be simpler and cheaper just to leave them at a rubbish dump – and it isn't as if our deceased friends and relatives would care! Yet we all know that such treatment of a

---

9 "I had to eat a piece of my friend to survive. It was repugnant", *The Sun*, 13 October 2012, http://www.thesun.co.uk/sol/homepage/features/4587280/Plane-crash-survivor-who-ate-the-flesh-of-dead-passengers-to-stay-alive-has-defended-his-actions-40-years-to-the-day-since-Andes-disaster.html

corpse would be wrong. We regard a human body, dead or alive, as much more than what the scientific worldview would tell us it is.

Our feelings about cannibalism not only reflect our attitude towards the human body, even in death. They also show our implicit awareness that the pleasure of eating has a certain natural purpose. Why do we shudder at the thought of eating a human kidney, yet feel unperturbed at the thought of receiving a kidney transplant? At least part of the answer is surely that we *enjoy* eating. We delight in the taste of food and we enjoy the sensations of swallowing hearty mouthfuls and relieving hunger. The thought of taking such pleasure in ingesting part of a fellow human being is ghoulish. At some level we recognise that pleasure too – even mere physical pleasure – has a *meaning*. In other words, it has a certain (intrinsic) purpose. It is right to take pleasure in eating proper food, and wrong to take pleasure in eating what should never serve as food. The cannibal family in *The Texas Chainsaw Massacre* delight in eating other human beings, and this delight is in one way even more horrific than their sheer homicidal brutality. It is a monstrous perversion of the true purpose of the pleasure of eating.

Sexual pleasure and its abuse

We will now turn to the subject of sex. In the first chapter, we claimed that sex has three natural purposes: pleasure, the celebration of romantic love and the generation of new life. We suggested, moreover, that these purposes are connected. When loving, pleasurable sexual union leads to pregnancy and childbirth, we may properly speak of 'love giving birth to love'. The celebration of love is inseparable from the sheer physical ecstasy of the act. Likewise, procreation and family life are the natural *consummation* of romantic love, not merely an accidental by-product of it. At this point, however, we wish to approach this whole topic from a different angle. We have seen that it makes good sense to speak of the natural purpose *of pleasure* – even of mere physical pleasure. Pleasure itself is undoubtedly one of nature's purposes but, often, it also serves some further purpose. We have also seen that it is possible to abuse pleasure, even the humble pleasure of eating. Our guiding question now is: what counts as an abuse of sexual pleasure?

It is obvious that the purely physical side of sexual pleasure is not simply an end in itself. When a couple in love have sex, they celebrate their love precisely *through* giving each other physical pleasure. The celebration of romantic love is one of the purposes of sexual pleasure. Infidelity is not only a betrayal of one's partner; it is a misuse of sexual pleasure. Again, Josef Fritzl's abuse of his daughter was a perverted fulfilment of a natural and, in itself, healthy desire for sexual intimacy and pleasure. It was perverted, because rape and incest are not what sexual pleasure is *for*. Not only did he inflict severe harm on his daughter, but he abused *his own* sexuality in fathering children with her.

However, the celebration and affirmation of sexual love cannot be the sole purpose of sexual pleasure. Since reproduction too is one thing that sex is for, it surely follows that sexual pleasure has an intrinsically meaningful connection with reproduction. It too is one of the things that sexual pleasure is for. This does not just mean that sexual pleasure is a highly effective spur to propagating one's species. A man and a woman striving to have a child can take all the more joy in their sexual union *because* they hope it will lead to pregnancy.

What makes coitus special

In chapter one we said that the biological connection between coitus and reproduction endows coitus with a significance it would otherwise lack. It reveals something about the meaning and purpose of coitus. This implies that coitus is a special kind of sex act. Even without thinking about its biological connection with reproduction, no one would deny that coitus *is* a special kind of sex act. It has a special meaning that other sex acts lack. Some religious traditions treat it as the *only* appropriate celebration of sexual love and some couples, both religious and non-religious, choose not to engage in any other kind of sexual intimacy. Even the crude analogy sometimes drawn between sexual relations and baseball recognises the special place of coitus by calling it a 'home run'.

Why do we naturally and unthinkingly regard it as special? To begin with, it has a unique mutuality. If we consider the sheer physical pleasure of sex, coitus is the only form of sexual activity in which the man gives the woman this pleasure in the very same act by which she gives it to him. In every other kind of sex act, one party gives physical pleasure to the other, who (in some cases) may simultaneously reciprocate, but need not do so. At the level of physical pleasure, coitus is uniquely egalitarian. Furthermore, coitus is the only sex act, apart from anal intercourse, that involves penile penetration, a hugely powerful symbol and expression of loving union. However, the obvious association of the anus with the most physically repellent of all bodily functions unavoidably colours acts of anal intercourse. A heterosexual man who *preferred* anal to vaginal intercourse would be thought odd at best and perverse at worst. He would be abusing his capacity for sexual pleasure.

In more ways than one, then, coitus naturally holds pride of place among sex acts. It is no accident that it alone is given the name "copulation", which literally means something like 'union'. Coitus gives richer expression to loving sexual union than any other kind of sex act. Can it then be an accident that it is also the only sex act that can lead to pregnancy and childbirth – the only act of love that can give birth to love? Nature has made coitus both the supreme expression of sexual love and the natural means by which this love blossoms into family love. This suggests that the two primary meanings of sex (love and reproduction) are not naturally meant to be separated. Sexual acts that by their nature cannot lead to reproduction are also, by their nature, less powerful expressions of love than the one sexual act that *can* naturally lead to reproduction.

Sexual love lived to the full

We argued in chapter one that there can really be no such thing as 'casual sex'. Much as we might sometimes wish to pretend otherwise, at some level we know that *every* sexual act is significant in a way that is not true, for instance, of every act of eating or drinking. In general, it is an abuse of sexual pleasure to act as if this were not the case. We now suggest that the meaningful connection of sex with reproduction must be one reason for this. Human sexuality exists, fundamentally, for the sake of the generation of new human life. And the generation of new human life is a graver and more wonderful thing than words can express. It is hardly surprising, then, that we should feel there is something inescapably special about everything directly connected with our sexuality. This, in turn, gives us additional reason to conclude that the two primary purposes of sex are not naturally meant to be separated.

Reproduction is one of the intrinsic purposes of human sexuality. It is one of the *meanings* of human sexuality. Several things follow from this. To begin with, it follows that a loving sexual relationship between a man and a woman is, in a way, incomplete if they commit to each other but decide never to have children. A voluntarily childless couple do not experience the full meaning, and the full joy, of their own sexuality. Their sex life is a celebration of romantic love, but this love is not given the opportunity to grow into full-fledged family love.

The natural family needs support

Of course, the desire of some couples not to have children is understandable. Having children is a daunting prospect. For the woman, pregnancy is burdensome and childbirth painful, sometimes even dangerous. The first year or two of a child's life means more or less constant stress and sleeplessness for both parents. The financial costs of housing, feeding, clothing and schooling a child can be crippling for poorer couples. And the emotional strains of childrearing are readily imaginable to anyone, though perhaps not fully comprehensible except to parents themselves. Fans of *The Simpsons* will remember the episode in which a young, unmarried Marge learns that she is pregnant. Having broken the news to her, a cheerful Doctor Hibbert hands her an information pamphlet for first-time expectant mothers entitled "So You've Ruined Your Life". Even couples who yearn to have children can appreciate the joke.

The difficulties of childrearing mean that a couple planning to have children cannot do it alone. They need the support, both material and emotional, of friends and family. But they also need the support of society at large. Employers must be understanding about some of their female employees needing to take maternity leave and, more generally, about the special stresses and strains that parenthood places on both male and female employees. Childcare centres and schools deserve government support, and it is appropriate that couples with children receive other forms of government support, such as tax concessions and grants.

More basically, couples who have or plan to have children deserve *societal respect* for the path they have taken. Society should not send young men and women the message that having children means "ruining your life".

It is not even enough that society should respect the decision to have children, without treating it as deserving of any special praise. We would reiterate what we said above: bringing new life into the world is an incomparably greater act than any other of which human beings are capable. Even apart from the huge burdens and sacrifices that childrearing entails, the choice to have children deserves special honour. Young men and women are really being cheated if they are told, in effect, that the choice not to have children for the sake of pursuing a successful and lucrative career is every bit as praiseworthy as the choice to have children, even if this means endangering one's career and financial prospects. By sending this message, society is denying childrearing the honourable place it truly deserves in any sane scheme of values, and it is making life harder than it has to be for young people who are contemplating becoming parents.

Why we need marriage

This brings us back to the topic of marriage. We have already observed that one good reason for having an institution like marriage is the wild character of human sexual desire. Most human beings naturally long for a lasting, exclusive sexual relationship with one other person, yet they also naturally have hugely powerful and indiscriminate sexual desires, whose satisfaction would spell disaster for genuine romantic love. Part of the solution to this problem is for a loving couple to make a formal, solemn commitment to each other. We may now add that, given the awesome responsibility and burden of childrearing, a loving couple who want children have still more reason to make such a formal commitment. In the first place, single parenthood is far more burdensome than shared parenthood. If a man and a woman conceive a child together, it is unfair for only one of them to be saddled with all of the burdens of raising him or her – and unfair to the child as well.

A solemn vow not to abandon one's partner when the going gets tough is thus even more important if a couple is planning to have children than if they are not. In the second place, if a couple intent on children are to receive the various kinds of support they urgently need, they have to give formal, *public* notice of their intention. Marriage has traditionally served this purpose. Weddings are, after all, meant to be public events. The spouses are not just pledging themselves to each other; they are giving notice to society at large that they are doing so – and they are publicly asking for help and support, above all in their future childrearing. Support for prospective or actual parents begins with the social and legal recognition of marriage.

Some people resist the idea of a loving couple making a public, legally recognised commitment to each other. Isn't love something fundamentally private and not society's or the government's business? And, more importantly, isn't *freedom* essential to a healthy, loving relationship? It can seem as if the institution of marriage spoils love by taking away a couple's freedom. What should be a spontaneous union of hearts suddenly becomes instead a coldly contractual relationship. From this point of view, the push for legal recognition of same-sex marriage is actually bad for same-sex couples. It would be better to fight for the abolition of marriage as an institution! But we think this is a superficial view. It is normal and healthy for committed lovers to want public recognition, affirmation and support for their life as a couple. And while it is true that marriage involves a real sacrifice of freedom, this in no way means that marriage spoils romantic love.

> *(John) When my mum was in her mid-twenties she didn't want to get married. When it was suggested to her that maybe she ought to marry, she was quite angry. As far as she was concerned, there was no way she could spend the rest of her life with one man. However, 33 years and 11 kids later, she is still married to my dad. If anyone asks her to rate her marriage out of ten, she says "eleven". And she isn't kidding. I first asked her to rate it out of ten in 2005 and the answer has*

been the same every time I have asked her since. When I ask her why she changed her mind about marriage, she usually points to my dad. The one time she really explained to me why she changed her mind she said something I'll never forget. "Marriage is a package deal and I knew it was for life. You take everything with it, the good and the bad. What I lost in freedom is nothing compared to what I've gained both qualitatively and quantitatively. On a human level the good we have gained from our staying together vastly outweighs the suffering there has been." My dad says the same thing but in a different way. As he puts it, "there must be some sacrifice of a good if you are to gain an even greater good in return". He says he is more in love with my mum than when they first got married.

Married without children?

A childless couple, we have said, misses out on the full meaning, and the full joy, of their own sexuality. If a man and woman both want children but prove unable to conceive, this is a real tragedy. However, if a couple deliberately *avoid* ever having children, they are voluntarily depriving themselves of one of the goods connected with sexuality – indeed, of an incomparably great good. They are voluntarily *preventing* their relationship from flowering into the fullness of family life.

As we have noted, reflection on coitus suggests that nature intends the two meanings of sex (romantic love and children) not to be separated. By deliberately and *permanently* separating them, a couple is at the very least opting for a fundamentally different kind of relationship than they would have if they were open, in principle, to children. A relationship whose basis is romantic love open to childbirth is radically different from one whose basis is romantic love that is wilfully closed to this possibility. We would go so far as to say that preferring a relationship without children to one with children means refusing to live in full harmony with nature. It means refusing to embrace the natural goodness of sexual love in its full richness. But it means more than this. Permanently separating the pleasure of sex from one of its purposes, reproduction, is like separating the pleasure of eating from its natural purpose, nourishment. It represents a misunderstanding of what human sexuality is *for*.

Here it might be objected that, after all, a loving couple who choose not to have children still recognise and respect the other great natural purpose of human sexuality, the celebration of romantic love. In one way this is certainly true. Yet, in another way, severing the celebration of romantic love from its natural connection with reproduction impoverishes even romantic love itself. We remarked earlier that a child is quite literally a living embodiment of his or her parents' loving union. An act of sexual love has brought the child into being, and he or she is the flesh and blood of both parents. Thereafter, even if the parents should cease to love each other, the child they have brought into the world is a bond between them that they can share with no one else, even if they wanted to.

Again, when they have a child, a couple have a shared object of new love and a shared responsibility to rear him or her. We all know that love and affection of every kind flourish best when two people care about the same things and have common tasks. People become friends because of such things as a shared interest in sport or comics. Deep friendships often form when people work together on something they are passionate about, such as a political campaign or a scientific study. What could bring two people closer together than the monumental task of rearing the child they love?

Love of all kinds is essentially about *giving*. The more one loves, the more one wants to give. A loving couple who wish to share their love with their children understand better what love is all about than a loving couple who take pains to avoid having children. The choice to separate the pleasure of sex from its reproductive purpose reflects a sadly limited understanding of its other purpose, the celebration of romantic love.

Same-sex marriage: in harmony with nature?

If it is true that the two purposes of human sexuality, love and reproduction, should not be separated, what does this mean for same-sex couples? While a same-sex couple cannot have children together, they can of course adopt children. Alternatively, one of the partners can have a child by means of a sperm donor, IVF, or a surrogate mother, and the couple can then raise this child together. Many same-sex couples certainly do raise children, or wish to do so. Might we then say that a loving same-sex couple who raise a child respect the two purposes of human sexuality in the only way they can? Their sexual intimacy cannot lead to pregnancy, but they want to raise children together and there are opportunities for them to do so. Are they not then living in harmony with nature?

We have emphasised the intrinsic *meaningfulness* of the connection between coitus and reproduction. The connection endows coitus with a unique significance. No sex act between two men or two women can have the character of 'love giving birth to love'. A same-sex relationship cannot have the full richness that a heterosexual relationship can have. Moreover, a child raised by a same-sex couple cannot be the living embodiment of the couple's loving sexual union. We remarked above that it is natural to desire not only to raise children but to *have* children. Moreover, it is natural to desire to conceive children with one's life-partner. Same-sex partners cannot satisfy this natural desire.

Of course it is possible to love a child who is not one's own flesh and blood, just as it is possible for a child to love an adoptive parent. But this does not mean that biological parentage is unimportant. Adopted children often wish to know the identity of their biological parents, and children who learn late in life that they were adopted are normally shocked at the news. When a man discovers that he is not in fact the father of the child he has loved and raised as his own for years, he is invariably devastated. These feelings are not irrational. We all recognise that the relation of parent to child is intrinsically significant. Certainly, there are terrible cases where removing a child from his or her biological parents may be in the child's best interests, and there is no reason why a child cannot have a stable and happy upbringing with adoptive parents. But, other things being equal, it is much the best thing for a child to be brought up by his or her mother and father.

Some scientists have recently claimed that, within a few years, it may be possible to convert male stem cells into female gametes, and female stem cells into male gametes. Lab technicians could then, in principle, create a viable embryo out of genetic material from two men or two women. In this way, same-sex couples *could* have children biologically related to both partners. However, even if this process (known as "*in vitro* gametogenesis") were to succeed, it would remain true that children so conceived would not be the fruit of loving sexual intercourse. The connection between sex and reproduction would still be broken and there would be no 'love giving birth to love'.

Suppose that a bisexual man opts to form a relationship with another man and raise a child with him, when he might happily have formed a relationship with a woman and had children with her. If we accept that the natural connection between sex and reproduction is intrinsically meaningful and deserves respect, we could hardly say that *he* pays it due respect. He is not living in harmony with nature. Like a heterosexual man who gets married with every intention of *never* having children, this bisexual man would be wilfully refusing to embrace the full natural goodness of sexual love. It might seem that the case is different with men and women who are exclusively homosexual. Such people cannot enter into a loving heterosexual relationship, even if they wished to do so. If they form a loving same-sex relationship and raise children with their partners, they are not *wilfully* refusing to embrace the full natural goodness of sexual love. Nonetheless, it would surely be stretching the truth to say that their lives are properly in harmony with the natural purposes of sex.

But same-sex attraction is natural!

Some readers may protest that, after all, same-sex attraction is itself something natural. How could it be 'unnatural' to act on one's natural desires? Here we need to make a distinction between two senses of 'natural'. On the non-nihilist view of nature we have faintly and incompletely sketched, not everything that happens 'naturally' can be said to be 'natural', in the sense of being in harmony with nature's *purposes*. We would follow Aristotle in saying that nature sometimes 'aims' at something, but misses its mark.

When a pregnancy miscarries, as we remarked in the last chapter, this represents a terrible failure on nature's part. When a baby is born without pain receptors, this is likewise a serious natural failure. Human beings urgently need the capacity to feel pain and the lack of pain receptors is in a real sense 'unnatural', even though the physiological processes that result in this catastrophe are in one obvious sense perfectly 'natural'. Again, a human being who suffers from the medical condition sometimes called pica (the desire to eat non-nutritive substances like metal or sand) has a disordered, unnatural appetite. No doubt this disorder sometimes has a physiological basis, such as mineral deficiency. The causal history of the condition could in principle be traced and would, in the same obvious sense, be quite 'natural'. Nonetheless, the condition itself is 'unnatural', in the sense that it conflicts with nature's purposes.

Reproduction is one of the essential natural purposes of sex. A desire for a kind of sexual intimacy that is intrinsically unapt for reproduction might indeed be 'natural', in the first sense. However, it would certainly be 'unnatural', in the second sense. It would not be in line with nature's purposes.

(Jeremy) *It may sound heartless to describe a person's sexual orientation as 'unnatural'. Yet, even when I considered myself exclusively homosexual, I could not help sometimes wishing, or half-wishing, that I was not. In other words, I was half-inclined to see my own sexuality as 'unnatural', even if I would not have used that word. The thought that I would never be able to have a romantic relationship with a woman made me sad, though I hardly dared admit it to myself. And even while I was in a long-term same-sex relationship, I could never quite convince myself that my partner and I were really just like any straight couple. We had a happy home life together and we both hoped this would last our whole lives. All the same, the slogan "equal but different" never sat comfortably with me. I did not draw any conscious connection between this vague unease and the impossibility of my partner and I ever having children together, but in retrospect I believe this was at least one reason for it.*

Marriage and the law

Marriage, as we said at the outset, is indeed all about love. But there are different kinds of love. With reference to coitus leading to reproduction, we have spoken of 'love giving birth to love'. This kind of love – romantic love that, through coitus, blossoms naturally into family love – is the richest possible fulfilment of the possibilities of human sexuality. Moreover, an exclusive heterosexual partnership provides the only setting for begetting and rearing children that *in every way* respects the profound significance of the biological bond between parent and child. For both these reasons, we suggest, it is appropriate that the term 'marriage' not be applied indiscriminately to heterosexual and homosexual unions. Reserving its application to heterosexual unions is a way of acknowledging that, whatever else may be said about homosexual unions, their intrinsic unaptness for reproduction makes them radically different from heterosexual unions.

Supporters of same-sex marriage sometimes ask why same-sex couples should not be *allowed* to marry. This way of framing the question is, however, misleading. Same-sex couples have for decades been allowed to celebrate their love physically, to live together and, if they wish, to go through ceremonies in which a celebrant pronounces them 'married'. Even the right to raise children was granted to same-sex couples in many jurisdictions long before same-sex marriage become a hot-button political issue. What is at stake in the same-sex marriage debate is not the *permission* to do anything. It is rather the legal *recognition* of exclusive same-sex partnerships as 'marriages'.

Legal recognition is largely a matter of symbolism. Supporters of same-sex marriage are asking for a symbolic affirmation that exclusive, loving homosexual unions are not in any important way different from exclusive, loving heterosexual unions. At the time of writing, this recognition has been granted in The Netherlands, Belgium, Canada, Spain, South Africa, Norway, Sweden, Argentina, Iceland, Portugal, Denmark, Brazil, England and Wales, France, New Zealand, Uruguay, Luxembourg, Scotland, and Ireland. A majority of U.S. states recognise same-sex marriage and, in the wake of the 2015 Obergefell decision, more are likely to follow. Finland has passed a law recognising same-sex marriage, which will come into effect in 2017. In the Western world, at any rate, the push for same-sex marriage has been hugely successful.

Nonetheless, we maintain that legal recognition of same-sex marriage is misguided. Heterosexual and homosexual unions *are*, in fact, importantly different. A sexual relationship that can naturally lead to children is fundamentally different from one that cannot. Marriage legislation should symbolically affirm this difference by reserving the term "marriage" for heterosexual unions.

What about autonomy and equality?

Defenders of same-sex marriage argue that legal recognition of same-sex marriage is a simple matter of respect for autonomy and equality. If the government does not allow homosexual men and women to marry, it unjustly violates their autonomy. Furthermore, it refuses to acknowledge that same-sex and opposite-sex romantic unions are equal. We have argued that, in fact, there is no question of governments *allowing* homosexuals to marry. If part of what is distinctive about the institution historically called "marriage" is that the married couple's sexual intimacy may lead to children, then it is *physically impossible* for two men or two women to marry. There is no sense in speaking of a 'right' to do the impossible.

As for equality, we are indeed saying that same-sex and opposite-sex unions are in one respect 'unequal'. "Love giving birth to love" is impossible within a same-sex union, and possible within an opposite-sex one. But this 'inequality' is an undeniable fact. We have sought to explain why we also believe it to be a morally significant fact. The institution of marriage should respect this fact and its moral significance.

What about infertile couples?

A common objection to the view of marriage we have proposed is that it seems to rule out marriage for infertile couples. An infertile opposite-sex couple cannot have children, any more than a same-sex couple can. Yet no one has ever argued that infertile couples cannot (or should not) marry. Isn't there a double standard here? We don't think so. We have already emphasised that there is a world of difference between an infertile opposite-sex couple and a *voluntarily* childless (though fertile), opposite-sex couple. A man and a woman who *deliberately* destroy the natural connection between their sex life and all possibility of procreation are refusing to live in harmony with nature.

A couple who are too old to conceive or who want children but prove unable to conceive naturally are still living in harmony with nature. Their sex life is naturally geared to procreation and they do not systematically *avoid* pregnancy. In the case of young but infertile couples, nature has, sadly, 'missed its mark'. By contrast, a same-sex couple engage in sexual activity that is in no sense naturally geared to procreation. Their sex life therefore lacks the procreative meaning that is present in the sex life even of an infertile, opposite-sex couple. This meaning, we have urged, is the proper basis of the institution of marriage.

We think that homosexuals too can acknowledge the special meaning of sex leading to pregnancy. They need not insist that a

loving homosexual union is simply 'equal' to a loving heterosexual
one.

> *(Jeremy) At the time I first thought about the significance of*
> *the connection between coitus and reproduction, I still considered*
> *myself exclusively homosexual. Thinking about this connection*
> *certainly did not make me feel differently about other men. I still*
> *found men sexually attractive and, moreover, I still longed for a*
> *loving relationship with another man. Even after I had rediscovered*
> *an interest in women, my homosexual desires did not simply*
> *vanish. For a long time, my feelings for one of my (heterosexual)*
> *male friends were deeply coloured with sexual desire. On one*
> *occasion, after an unsuccessful date with a woman, I found myself*
> *thinking about this male friend with such love and longing that*
> *it brought me to tears. All the same, since first being struck by*
> *the special (procreative) character of heterosexual unions, I have*
> *never doubted that they are basically and importantly different*
> *from homosexual ones.*

If, as we have argued, there is such a thing as living 'in
harmony with nature', the difference between these two kinds
of relationship is profoundly important. Since it is right that
governments should support men and women who wish to
commit themselves to a relationship likely to lead to children,
it is also right that governments should symbolically affirm the
uniqueness of this relationship. To do so is not to deny the
reality of homosexual love, let alone the humanity and dignity of
homosexuals. It is to affirm the specialness of love that can give
birth to love.

Two Men talk about Marriage
Summary of the Argument

1

- Sex expresses, as nothing else can, the special love of spouses for each other. This is why sexual exclusivity matters in marriage.
- Even a single act of sexual infidelity, however casual in spirit, does damage to a marriage. Why is this? It cannot be simply because the spouses have promised never to be unfaithful. They make the promise only because sexual fidelity is important anyway.
- The meaning of sexual infidelity is not up to the parties involved. Sex has a meaning beyond our control. Our feelings about public nudity and sex reflect this.
- The intrinsic meaning of sex means that there is no such thing as 'casual sex'.
- We want sexually exclusive relationships, but sexual exclusivity often goes against the grain. This is why a formal promise of exclusivity is important – one reason why the institution of marriage exists.
- The natural connection between sex and reproduction adds a further dimension to the intrinsic meaning of sex. Coitus leading to reproduction may fairly be described as 'love giving birth to love'.
- This means that part of the natural *purpose* of sex is reproduction.

2

- Sex, we are saying, has an intrinsic meaning – a *natural* purpose. But what does it mean to speak of 'natural' meaning or purpose?

- Science tells us nothing about the 'meaning' or 'purpose' of things. A purely scientific view of the world has no place for meaning and purpose.

- Human beings recognise the reality of meaning and purpose. They are 'spiritual' beings, unlike non-human animals.

- Human sexuality reflects human spirituality.

- We need a worldview that makes room for human spirituality. Hence, we need a worldview based on more than science.

- A worldview that makes room for human spirituality must recognise that some things are *naturally* good, and that nature somehow *aims* at goodness (even if it sometimes misses). Though it may sound strange, this way of thinking is, in fact, familiar to all of us.

- On this understanding of nature, it makes sense to speak of living 'in harmony with nature' or 'according to nature'.

3

- Physical pleasure has a natural purpose or 'meaning'. This is true even of such humble pleasures as that of eating.
- The natural purposes of sexual pleasure are the celebration of romantic love and the generation of new life. These purposes are connected.
- It follows that coitus is a uniquely important form of sexual intimacy, as most people intuitively recognise.
- We should not deliberately separate the two naturally connected purposes of sexual pleasure. To do so is to fail to live 'in harmony with nature'.
- The stresses and strains of childrearing make it all the more important that an opposite-sex couple make a formal commitment to stay together through thick and thin.
- Family life needs governmental and societal support. This means that (traditional) marriage needs governmental and societal support.
- Same-sex couples cannot have children together, which makes their relationships fundamentally different from those of opposite-sex couples.
- Same-sex attraction is 'natural' in one sense, but not in another. It is not something at which nature can be said to 'aim'.
- Legal recognition of same-sex marriage is a symbolic affirmation that opposite-sex unions and same-sex unions are not importantly different. But they are.
- Governments ought to reserve the term "marriage" to opposite-sex unions.

Bibliography

Newspaper Articles

"Husband Sued by Wife for Lack of Sex", *Sydney Morning Herald*, 6 September 2011, http://www.smh.com.au/ lifestyle/life/husband-sued-by-wife-for-lack-of-sex-20110905-1juqw.html

"I had to eat a piece of my friend to survive. It was repugnant", *The Sun*, 13 October 2012, http://www. thesun.co.uk/sol/homepage/features/4587280/Plane-crash-survivor-who-ate-the-flesh-of-dead-passengers-to-stay-alive-has-defended-his-actions-40-years-to-the-day-since-Andes-disaster.html

"What is love? Five theories on the greatest emotion of all", *The Guardian*, 13 December 2012, http://www. theguardian.com/commentisfree/2012/dec/13/what-is-love-five-theories

Books

Black Elk (1989) *The Sacred Pipe: Black Elk's Account of the Seven Rites of the Oglala Sioux*, Brown, J. E. (ed.), Norman: University of Oklahoma Press.

Einstein, A. (1954) *Ideas and Opinions*, New York: Crown Publishers. (1979)

Albert Einstein, The Human Side: New Glimpses from His Archives, Dukas, H & Hoffmann. B (eds.) Princeton, N.J. & Chichester, West Sussex: Princeton University Press.

Sagan, C. (1997) *The Demon-Haunted World: Science as a Candle in the Dark*, London: Headline.

Schrödinger, E. (1954) *Nature and the Greeks*, Cambridge: Cambridge University Press.

Other

Ryan, C. (2014) "Is Monogamy Unnatural?", talk given at Sydney Opera House on 28 June 2014, transcript available at: http://www.abc.net.au/radionational/programs/scienceshow/is-monogamy-unnatural3f/5516302#transcript

About the Authors

Jeremy Bell has completed an M.Phil in philosophy at the University of Sydney and a Ph.D. in philosophy at the University of Chicago. He is presently a casual lecturer and tutor in history and philosophy at Campion College Australia. He became a Catholic in 2012 after many years as a non-believer.

John McCaughan has a Bachelor of Arts from the University of Notre Dame Australia, majoring in history and English. He was first employed as a professional writer overseas and is currently working in the NSW Public Sector. He lists his parents' marriage as the biggest influence on his life followed closely by his seven brothers and three sisters.

OTHER CONNOR COURT TITLES

BIOETHICS AT THE CROSSROAD OF RELIGIONS

Thoughts on the Foundations of Bioethics in
Christianity and Islam

Antoine Tarabay

Foreword by Cardinal George Pell

ISBN: 9781925138672

Paperback, 198 pages, Price: $29.95

ABOUT BIOETHICS - VOLUME 4: MOTHERHOOD, EMBODIED LOVE AND CULTURE

Nicholas Tonti-Filippini

ISBN: 9781922168603

Paperback, 480 pagesPrice: $39.95

MANUAL OF CATHOLIC MEDICAL ETHICS

Responsible Healthcare from a Catholic Perspective

Editors: WJ Eijk MD, LM Hendriks, JA Raymakers

ISBN: 9781925138160

Hardback, 720 pages, $79.95

To order visit:

www.connorcourt.com